31 Prayers for Courage

Nathaniel Turner

Copyright © 2011 Nathaniel Turner

All rights reserved.

ISBN: 1461173914
ISBN-13: 978-1461173915

Scripture taken from the NEW AMERICAN STANDARD BIBLE®, Copyright © 1960,1962,1963,1968,1971,1972,1973,1975,1977,1995 by The Lockman Foundation. Used by permission.

DEDICATION

To all those whom fear has hindered from their pursuit of the Lord.

CONTENTS

Acknowledgments	i
Author's Note	iii
Courage When Facing Difficulty	1
Courage to Fear God	11
Courage When Facing Others	15
Courage to Remember God's Promises	21
Courage When Needing to Be Rescued	29
Courage When Facing Spiritual Battles	33
Courage When Facing Spiritual Opposition	43
Courage When Troubled by Temptation and Sin	55
Courage When Facing Uncertainty	59
Courage When Feeling Weak	73
Courage in Tribulation	81

ACKNOWLEDGMENTS

My gratitude goes to God, above all. *Gratias ago*, too, to my father, without whom this would never have been conceived, and to my wife, whose encouragement kept me going.

AUTHOR'S NOTE

What I have written here is meant to help the reader vocalize his or her prayers to the Lord directed by the Word of God. I have introduced each prayer with the phrase, "Dear Lord," and finished them with the phrase, "In Thy Son's Name I pray, AMEN," which is my own custom. Both the prayers themselves and the introductory and concluding words are meant to be a guide only; feel free to supplement or alter these prayers for your personal use.

It is my intention that these prayers assist the reader in his or her personal prayer life and help him or her to speak to God when he or she cannot find the words. If the reader does wish to pray publicly what I have written here, I would appreciate a mention that it was I who wrote it.

Please feel free to visit the 31 Prayers website at
http://www.31Prayers.com
to find out about future installments in the 31 Prayers series and to post your comments and questions about this book.

COURAGE WHEN FACING DIFFICULTY

Genesis 46:3

He said, "I am God, the God of your father; do not be afraid to go down to Egypt, for I will make you a great nation there."

Dear Lord,

    I have a great and daunting task before me. I fear the difficulty of the task, or the vulnerable position it may put me in. This is my journey to Egypt. Protect me on this journey, as You protected Jacob. God, You Who have always been there for me, as You were for Jacob, and for his father Isaac, and for his father Abraham. Make me a great nation, O LORD: reward me in this task that I may bring You glory before all people.

    In Thy Son's Name I pray, AMEN.

Deuteronomy 1:21

"See, the LORD your God has placed the land before you; go up, take possession, as the LORD, the God of your fathers, has spoken to you. Do not fear or be dismayed."

Dear Lord,

You have set a task before me, a calling to do Your will. Help me not to fear the dangers in the task, but to go up in confidence and to take possession of the land You have placed before me, which You have promised to me. Let me not fear or be dismayed, but let me be bold and courageous that You may be glorified.

In Thy Son's Name I pray, AMEN.

I Chronicles 28:20

Then David said to his son Solomon, "Be strong and courageous, and act; do not fear nor be dismayed, for the LORD God, my God, is with you. He will not fail you nor forsake you until all the work for the service of the house of the LORD is finished."

Dear Lord,

I am Your servant. I work for Your glory. Yet I fear the obstacles in my path; I do not know what may come against me, or worse still, I know it and I cannot withstand it. Help me, O God, to be as Your servant David commanded his son Solomon to be: let this young spark of wisdom for the wisest of Your people fill my heart and mind also. Let me be strong and courageous, O LORD, that I may act; let me not fear nor be dismayed, for the LORD God, You, the God of Abraham, Isaac, and Jacob, the God of King David and of the Prophets, Father of Jesus Christ my Savior, You are with me. Do not fail me or forsake me, O God, until the work for the service of Your house is finished.

In Thy Son's Name I pray, AMEN.

Ezra 10:4

"Arise! For this matter is your responsibility, but we will be with you; be courageous and act."

Dear Lord,

Though I am but a poor sinner, confessing my sins before you as Ezra once did, I have a great task for Your people and Your house. Help me to remember that others, members of Your body, O Christ, are with me, to support me, to pray for me, to build me up and to strengthen me; in the same way, help me to remember that You also are with me, since wherever two or more are gathered in Your Name, there You are also. Raise me up from this supplication that I may do Your will. This task is my responsibility, Father, but Your people, indeed You Yourself, through Your Holy Spirit, are with me. Help me to be courageous and act.

In Thy Son's Name I pray, AMEN.

COURAGE TO FEAR GOD

Exodus 20:20

Moses said to the people, "Do not be afraid; for God has come in order to test you, and in order that the fear of Him may remain with you, so that you may not sin."

Dear Lord,

I fear worldly things, my God. I fear elements of Your creation. Yet I ask for Your guidance; I ask that You come to me, as you came to the Israelites in the wilderness; I ask that You speak to me, not that I may die, for the Israelites feared death, but by dying You have conquered death, and by rising to new life, You have caused death itself to die. Rather, I ask that You speak to me so that, like Moses, I may fear not death but You, not creation but Creator, that I may not sin and that I may always live in faith, righteously, to Your glory.

In Thy Son's Name I pray, AMEN.

COURAGE WHEN FACING OTHERS

Genesis 50:19

But Joseph said to them, "Do not be afraid, for am I in God's place?"

Dear Lord,

Help me to remember, as Joseph reminded his brothers, that no man or woman is in Your place. Only You judge, O LORD, and whatever others may think or say about me and my decisions, only Your judgment matters to me, God. Help me to pursue You and Your will, turning away from my sin and embracing You, that You may judge me as righteous because of Your Son, Jesus Christ.

In Thy Son's Name I pray, AMEN.

Matthew 10:28

"Do not fear those who kill the body but are unable to kill the soul; but rather fear Him who is able to destroy both soul and body in hell."

Dear Lord,

I seek to be Your humble servant. Help me not to fear the judgment and consequences of those around me—my peers, my fellows, my mentors, or my boss. As the Pharisees did to Your Christ, others will curse and malign me for seeking to follow Your will. Your Truth is offensive to people of this world; help me not to fear their retribution, but let me fear instead Your strength, wisdom, power, and judgment. Help me to live in awe of you and, taking courage by Your Word, help me to follow only You.

In Thy Son's Name I pray, AMEN.

COURAGE TO REMEMBER GOD'S PROMISES

Joshua 1:9

"Have I not commanded you? Be strong and courageous! Do not tremble or be dismayed, for the LORD your God is with you wherever you go."

Dear Lord,

How forgetful I can be! You have told me before, writ in Your Word when You spoke to the Israelites, to Abraham, Isaac, and Jacob, to Moses, to Joshua, Your servants: I should not be afraid, because You go with me. No matter what opposition I face, You accompany me. Wherever I go, You are there; if I ascend to the heavens, or go down to the place of the dead; if I pursue the dawn in the east or the ends of the sea to the west; truly, even if I walk in the valley of the shadow of death, there You are to guide me and protect me, as you Promised Joshua and the Israelites as they entered the land which You had given over to them. Help me to remember these things, O LORD, and not to fear.

In Thy Son's Name I pray, AMEN.

Isaiah 41:13

*"For I am the LORD your God, who upholds your right hand,
Who says to you, 'Do not fear, I will help you.'"*

Dear Lord,

    I am often forgetful of Your promises; I do not recall how greatly You have helped me. In my flawed flesh, my memory of Your love and protection fails me. Remind me again, O LORD; collect again into my thoughts the acts of your lovingkindness. Tell me again Your Name, O LORD my God, the One Who is. You uphold my right hand; You give me strength to persevere. You say unto me, "Fear not," for You are with me; You help me, as You have helped me, as you helped my spiritual forefathers Abraham, Isaac, and Jacob. Guide me, O LORD, in the courage You bestow, that I may not forget Your faithfulness evermore.

    In Thy Son's Name I pray, AMEN.

Luke 12:7

"Indeed, the very hairs of your head are all numbered. Do not fear; you are more valuable than many sparrows."

Dear Lord,

You know and care for even the little sparrows; You protect their nests and You provide for them; You feed them and sustain them. Yet here am I, in the darkness of night, worrying about whether I shall live or die on the morrow. Father, guide me and remind me: You know me so well that You have numbered even the hairs upon my head. You know the dangers I face and You know, too, the outcomes. Give me the courage to trust in you, to hold fast to Your promises. For indeed, I am more valuable than many sparrows; how much more will you care for me than for one of these!

In Thy Son's Name I pray, AMEN.

COURAGE WHEN NEEDING TO BE RESCUED

Jeremiah 46:27

"But as for you, O Jacob My servant, do not fear,
Nor be dismayed, O Israel!
For, see, I am going to save you from afar,
And your descendants from the land of their captivity;
And Jacob will return and be undisturbed
And secure, with no one making him tremble."

Dear Lord,

    Let me not fear nor be dismayed, O God. I have been driven far from my home; I am no longer living near Your holy place. I am surrounded by sin and danger of my own making. My mistakes have led me astray, like Jonah, and like the Israelites cast into exile for their infidelity to you. Forgive me, Father, and guide me back into Your presence, as You promised the Israelites through the prophet Jeremiah: save me, though I am far from You, and rescue me and mine from the land of captivity. Help me to have courage in Your promise and strength in Your Word, for You are mightier than I, and by Your will may I be saved from that which I fear.

    In Thy Son's Name I pray, AMEN.

COURAGE WHEN FACING SPIRITUAL BATTLES

Deuteronomy 20:3-4

"He shall say to them, 'Hear, O Israel, you are approaching the battle against your enemies today. Do not be fainthearted. Do not be afraid, or panic, or tremble before them, for the LORD your God is the one who goes with you, to fight for you against your enemies, to save you.'"

Dear Lord,

A battle lies before me, O LORD. My enemies stand against me; they seek my life. Let me not be fainthearted. Let me not be afraid, nor panic, nor tremble before them, as You had Your priest direct the Israelites in the battle they faced. Help me to remember always that the LORD my God is the One Who goes with me. It is not I that fight in battle, but it is You that fight for me; You, the Creator of the universe and the Savior of man from himself, the Conqueror of sin and death, fight in my stead: who can stand against You? Remind me of this truth, O LORD.

In Thy Son's Name I pray, AMEN.

Deuteronomy 31:6

"Be strong and courageous, do not be afraid or tremble at them, for the LORD your God is the one who goes with you. He will not fail you or forsake you."

Dear Lord,

Lead me into the war for Your Promised Land. Many enemies lie before me, blocking my path to obedience to You. Cross the Jordan ahead of me, LORD; lead me into battle, that I may be courageous and without fear. Whether my enemies are men, opposed to Your will, or the very shortcomings of my own flesh and sin, or agents of the evil one, help me to lead my house, as Joshua led your people, into the Promised Land to possess it, just as You have commanded. For I know You will not fail or forsake me, but You will lead me to victory of my enemies for Your Name's sake.

In Thy Son's Name I pray, AMEN.

Joshua 8:1

Now the LORD said to Joshua, "Do not fear or be dismayed. Take all the people of war with you and arise, go up to Ai; see, I have given into your hand the king of Ai, his people, his city, and his land."

Dear Lord,

My foes are before me, LORD. I shall soon go up in battle against them. Help me not to fear or be dismayed. Bring to my mind those standing with me; perhaps relatives, parents, children, loved ones, friends, a church family or home. They will support me, fight alongside me. Give us all courage, for we are together in this war, we soldiers of Christ. Be with us as we go up against those that oppose Your will, as You were with Joshua and the Israelites. Give into our hand all that they possess, that they may know that You are God; let them not persist in persecution of Your Name and in opposition to Your will. To You be the glory and Your will be done, O LORD.

In Thy Son's Name I pray, AMEN.

II Chronicles 20:17

"'You need not fight in this battle; station yourselves, stand and see the salvation of the LORD on your behalf, O Judah and Jerusalem.' Do not fear or be dismayed; tomorrow go out to face them, for the LORD is with you."

Dear Lord,

Help me, O LORD, in my time of distress. Enemies approach me and face me, and I fear what may befall me. Help me to realize that the battle is not mine but Yours, O LORD, and that I do not fight in this battle, but You, Father, will fight, and indeed already have fought, and indeed already have won this battle. Help me to be strong and courageous and to trust in Your Name, for You are with me.

In Thy Son's Name I pray, AMEN.

COURAGE WHEN FACING SPIRITUAL OPPOSITION

Genesis 15:1

After these things the word of the LORD came to Abram in a vision, saying,

*"Do not fear, Abram,
I am a shield to you;
Your reward shall be very great."*

Dear Lord,

Help me not to fear. Be a shield for me, as You were for Abraham; protect me from fiery arrows. Help me, LORD, to see Your plan and to take courage in Your presence. Give unto me my reward, whether it is in this life, as with Abraham, or after I have passed from here into Your eternal kingdom.

In Thy Son's Name I pray, AMEN.

Joshua 10:24-25

When they brought these kings out to Joshua, Joshua called for all the men of Israel, and said to the chiefs of the men of war who had gone with him, "Come near, put your feet on the necks of these kings." So they came near and put their feet on their necks. Joshua then said to them, "Do not fear or be dismayed! Be strong and courageous, for thus the LORD will do to all your enemies with whom you fight."

Dear Lord,

You have long been on my side. You have won many battles for me and You have overcome many hardships on my behalf. Perhaps I have not been vigilant, perhaps I have not seen Your hand at work, but wherever I have succeeded, wherever I have overcome, You succeeded and You overcame first. You have shown me what happens to those who oppose Your will: they are frustrated, foiled, and defeated; they are led before Your soldiers in their defeat, and they are crushed underfoot, as Your Son crushed the head of the snake. They are tread upon and trampled as He in the Psalmist's prayer treads upon the lion and the cobra, tramples the young lion and the serpent. LORD, help me to see your work in my life, and help me to be courageous for the future.

In Thy Son's Name I pray, AMEN.

I Samuel 22:23

"Stay with me; do not be afraid, for he who seeks my life seeks your life, for you are safe with me."

Dear Lord,

I want to stay with You, close to You, that I may be protected by You. Your enemies have become my enemies since I have chosen to follow You, and they oppose me and seek to destroy me. They seek to ruin my life, whether by defamation, seduction, injury, or death. They have ruined others in Your house, like the priests of the LORD whom Saul killed because of David, the man after Your own heart. Protect me, LORD, for I will stay with You, as Abiathar son of Ahimelech son of Ahitub stayed with David and was safe there from Saul. Keep me safe from those who seek my life because of Your Name, O LORD.

In Thy Son's Name I pray, AMEN.

Psalm 27:3

*Though a host encamp against me,
My heart will not fear;
Though war arise against me,
In spite of this I shall be confident.*

Dear Lord,

I am a soldier in Your faithful army. You are my general, and it is for You and Your kingdom that I fight the enemy. That enemy opposes me and he opposes You; he has an army of his own and they seek to harm me through my work, my family, my church—sometimes by hurting those around me, sometimes by misleading them so that they hurt me. Whatever his tactics, I am faced with foes, openly seeking my pain. Yet I will not fear, I pray, and I will be confident. Help me to remember in these trying times that You have already won the war which rises against me; You have caused my adversaries to stumble and fall. Help me not to fear what has already fallen.

In Thy Son's Name I pray, AMEN.

Psalm 27:14

*Wait for the LORD;
Be strong and let your heart take courage;
Yes, wait for the LORD.*

Dear Lord,

I am under fire; my faith is attacked and I fear my destruction. Help me, LORD, to persevere. Help me to suffer with courage and strength, resolute in the hope you grant through grace. Help me, LORD, to persevere. It would be so easy to quit; it would be so easy to fall. Help me, LORD, to persevere. Yet I trust in You, hope in You, rely on You always. Help me, LORD, to persevere. Trouble surrounds me; enemies oppose me; weakness enters me; frailty turns me. Yet all this will fail, and my heart takes courage, for I believe that I will see the goodness of the LORD in the land of the living. Yes, I will wait for the LORD.

In Thy Son's Name I pray, AMEN.

COURAGE WHEN TROUBLED BY TEMPTATION AND SIN

Ruth 3:11

"Now, my daughter, do not fear. I will do for you whatever you ask, for all my people in the city know that you are a woman of excellence."

Dear Lord,

Heavenly Father, let me be counted among those who received You and were given the right to become Your children; let me be called "daughter" or "son" by You. Help me not to fear some shortcoming of mine or some rejection by You. Help me to be a person of excellence, known first to You, and second to Your people, that You may be glorified. Help me to remember that I ought not to fear Your judgment or retribution as long as I fear and respect and awe in You, O LORD. Guide me in Your love and truth.

In Thy Son's Name I pray, AMEN.

COURAGE WHEN FACING UNCERTAINTY

Psalm 9:9-10

The LORD also will be a stronghold for the oppressed,
A stronghold in times of trouble;
And those who know Your name will put their trust in You,
For You, O LORD, have not forsaken those who seek You.

Dear Lord,

I am oppressed and in a time of trouble; I want to put my trust in You, to seek You, that I may be unafraid. Be a stronghold for me, my God; save me from my distress. Help me to trust and to follow you, O LORD, all the days of my life. Do not forsake me or abandon me, for You are my one desire. Lead me forward, that I may excel in You and bring You glory, Father.

In Thy Son's Name I pray, AMEN.

Psalm 46:1-3

God is our refuge and strength,
A very present help in trouble.
Therefore we will not fear, though the earth should change
And though the mountains slip into the heart of the sea;
Though its waters roar and foam,
Though the mountains quake at its swelling pride.

Dear Lord,

Be my refuge and my strength, O God. For You are abundantly available, always present to help me in times of trouble. So I will not fear; help me not to fear anything which is under Your hand and Your eye. You have created everything, and so I will not fear when Your creation changes and turns by Your power, when the heights fall to the depths, bowing at Your feet, when the seas roar to proclaim Your glory and the very mountains tremble in awe of Your holiness. O LORD, help me to remember Your greatness, Your sovereignty, and hold fast to Your love and direction when the small problems of my life, dwarfed by the great movements of the earth, give me hardship. Help me always to lean on You.

In Thy Son's Name I pray, AMEN.

Isaiah 35:4

Say to those with anxious heart,
"Take courage, fear not.
Behold, your God will come with vengeance;
The recompense of God will come,
But He will save you."

Dear Lord,

My heart is anxious, O God; let it not be so. Say unto me to take courage and not to fear. Although I face opposition, and although it may seem that my enemies have achieved victories and won battles, tell me that You will come with vengeance, that Your recompense will come and that sin and injustice and death will be ended. You will save me. My heart is anxious, O God, but by your grace and guidance, I will take courage.

In Thy Son's Name I pray, AMEN.

Isaiah 41:10

"Do not fear, for I am with you;
Do not anxiously look about you, for I am your God.
I will strengthen you, surely I will help you,
Surely I will uphold you with My righteous right hand.'"

Dear Lord,

My future is uncertain. I do not know how I will be able to continue. I worry about tomorrow, O LORD. Help me to remember that You are with me. Help me not to cast about, searching in vain for help when You are my God, a reliable and steadfast safety for me. Give me Your strength; give me that certainty of Your help. Help me to consider the birds of the air as you uphold me with Your righteous right hand: help me to recall Your provision for all the needs of Your creation, and how much more you will provide for those who seek after You.

In Thy Son's Name I pray, AMEN.

Daniel 10:19

He said, "O man of high esteem, do not be afraid. Peace be with you; take courage and be courageous!" Now as soon as he spoke to me, I received strength and said, "May my lord speak, for you have strengthened me."

Dear Lord,

I am pained by weakness and fear. The future is daunting, and I am unsure of myself and my abilities. Give me strength by Your Word, as You gave to Your servant Daniel. You have gifted me with many things; let me use them wisely and to Your glory. O LORD, speak to me, guide me, direct me, command me; for You are my God and Savior, and it is from the blessing of Your mouth that I take courage.

In Thy Son's Name I pray, AMEN.

Luke 12:32

"Do not be afraid, little flock, for your Father has chosen gladly to give you the kingdom."

Dear Lord,

I must provide for my family, and yet I do not know from where my help will come. I worry about the future and I am wracked by the fear that tomorrow will not take care of itself. Help me to remember the lilies of the field, O LORD, how they grow: they neither toil nor spin, yet You have provided for them both nutrition and the clothing of their beauty, even though tomorrow they will be thrown into the furnace. If you care for something so small in Your creation, O God, how much more will You care for me! Help me not to fear tomorrow, regarding what I shall wear or what I shall eat or drink, but guide me to seek first Your kingdom, that these may be added unto me. For though we are as sheep to You, You have chosen gladly to give us Your kingdom. Give me that courage, LORD.

In Thy Son's Name I pray, AMEN.

COURAGE WHEN FEELING WEAK

II Kings 6:15-17

Now when the attendant of the man of God had risen early and gone out, behold, an army with horses and chariots was circling the city. And his servant said to him, "Alas, my master! What shall we do?" So he answered, "Do not fear, for those who are with us are more than those who are with them." Then Elisha prayed and said, "O LORD, I pray, open his eyes that he may see." And the LORD opened the servant's eyes and he saw; and behold, the mountain was full of horses and chariots of fire all around Elisha.

Dear Lord,

I can be blind without Your guidance; I can be foolish without Your wisdom. Help me not to be blind as the servant of Elisha, but grant that I may see and be courageous, knowing that there are more who are for me than against me. Help me to see and trust all the support, defense, protection, and salvation that You have provided for me. Send out Your horses, send out Your chariots of fire; surround me and shield me, that I may not falter or fail. Though others may come against me, You are with me: save my soul from distress and give me courage.

In Thy Son's Name I pray, AMEN.

Isaiah 43:1-2

But now, thus says the LORD, your Creator, O Jacob,
And He who formed you, O Israel,
"Do not fear, for I have redeemed you;
I have called you by name; you are Mine!

"When you pass through the waters, I will be with you;
And through the rivers, they will not overflow you.
When you walk through the fire, you will not be scorched,
Nor will the flame burn you."

Dear Lord,

You are my God, You alone; You created the heavens and the earth. You formed me in my mother's womb; You know me in my inmost being. I am but Your humble creation, O God. Alone, I am weak; but You are strong. You have redeemed me from my iniquity; You have cleansed me from my sin. Let me not fear vengeance, but let me put my faith in You and hope that I will be saved. You have called me by name and You have named me as Yours; could anything take me from Your hand? If, as the Israelites fleeing from the armies of Pharaoh, I pass through the waters, You will keep them from drowning me; if, as the sons of that rescued generation crossed over the Jordan, I seek the land You have promised, you will keep me from being swept away; if, as Your servants were compelled in the clutches of Babylon, I walk through the flames of the furnace of my enemies, let me not be scorched by the fire and let me be preserved to Your glory.

In Thy Son's Name I pray, AMEN.

Daniel 10:12

Then he said to me, "Do not be afraid, Daniel, for from the first day that you set your heart on understanding this and on humbling yourself before your God, your words were heard, and I have come in response to your words."

Dear Lord,

I pray to You humbly, O God. I am one of unclean lips, from a people of unclean lips; I am not worthy to untie the thong of Your sandal. I am weak and afraid, for I seek understanding of Your will for me, but I doubt that I am capable of carrying it out. Hear my words, O LORD, as you heard the words of Your servant Daniel, and give me strength to hear and to understand and to obey.

In Thy Son's Name I pray, AMEN.

COURAGE IN TRIBULATION

John 16:33

"These things I have spoken to you, so that in Me you may have peace. In the world you have tribulation, but take courage; I have overcome the world."

Dear Lord,

    I have great fear of the evils in this world. They have misused Your Word to incite riots and murders and wars. They have opposed Your Truth and oppressed Your people throughout the world, both socially and physically. They have sought out Your saints with a vengeance, to put them to death. They have brought forth false witness against You and Your followers, producing hatred and ill will against us among the ignorant people of this world. Your apostles they imprisoned, accused, tortured, and executed, only because they refused to be silent about Your Word. And they arrested Your Son, cursed Him, accused Him though He was blameless, mocked Him, spat upon Him, lashed Him, burdened Him, and crucified Him. How can I resist such evils, O God? How can I survive?

    But they have not been victorious, O LORD. Their heresies and deceptions have been cast into the light of Your Truth. Their oppression, however powerful, has never crushed the indomitable Holy Spirit, which breathes life into Your Church. The blood of the martyrs is the seed of the Church, and no matter how many evil has slain, so many more rise in their place. The lies have been cast out, the falsehoods have been revealed, and hatred has been turned away by love. Your apostles proclaimed Your Name to their dying breath, bringing countless more into the fold of believers. And Your Son, when He had died, descended into the depths and, harrowing hell itself, He broke the chains of sin and put death unto death; and when He had freed Your servants from the powers of sin and death, He was raised from the grave in triumph and He appeared to His disciples and He rose into Heaven; He sits at Your right hand, and indeed He will come again in glory to judge the living and the dead, and His kingdom will have no end!

    Help me, then, to take courage, O Heavenly Father; for no matter what tribulation I face in the world, You have already overcome it.

    In Thy Son's Name I pray, AMEN.

Made in the USA
Charleston, SC
19 August 2011